METAMORPHOSIS 2021

WHY NOT ME?

A Self-Help Therapy Book
from a Christian Perspective

by Dr. Kasona Coates

Copyright © 2023 by Dr. Kasona Coates

All rights reserved. No part of this publication may be reproduced, stored in retrieval systems, or transmitted, in any way or by any means, electronic, mechanical, photocopying, recording, or otherwise, without the prior written permission of the author.

ISBN: Paperback 979-8-218-30126-2
ISBN: Ebook 979-8-218-30125-5

Book Layout: Ravi Ramgati

Acknowledgements

This book is dedicated to my beautiful aunts Jean Newkirk-McRae and Josephine Carpenter who always encouraged me to tell my story. We all have one, but this is mine. To my natural and church family. To my children (Porcha & Rafael) and my beautiful grandchildren (Zariaha, Dominic, Kaitlyn, Amari, Isyss, Carter, Kholie, & RJ). My beautiful mother (Doris) and dad (Eschol). My loving and supportive husband (Ray). My awesome leaders, guides, mentors (Bishops James Stoudemire, Charles Wilson, Andrew Stephens, and Curtis Simmons). Special thanks to (Bishops Eugene Rice & Frankie Key) for providing me the Solid Foundation and the motivation to accomplish anything. Most of all, I thank God for my Lord and Savior Jesus Christ who has given me all my Help.

Preface

Everyone would like to have a hero. What is a hero? The dictionary defines a hero as a person who is admired or idealized for courage, outstanding achievements, or noble qualities. Then, there are different types of heroes such as Superman, Romeo from Romeo and Juliet, the Joker from Batman and Robbin, Mr. Darcy from the movie Pride and Prejudice, and finally the "underdog," the person that others counted out. The point is that everyone has a hero that has inspired them in some way. This book is the transformation that took place in Kasona's (the underdog) life by The unseen Hero.

Prayer

Lord, thank you to the person that is reading this book. Thank you for keeping them safely unto this point. Father, will you continue to guide them in the direction that they need to go. Lord, I pray that the words and activities in this book will benefit them in every way possible. Please give them grace and mercy as they proceed so that they may be strengthened where they are weak. Most of all, when they arrive at the destination of the book, let the book do what it was intended to do, which is uplift and inspire in Jesus' name, Amen.

Introduction

Run Kasona! Run! Do not quit! I can't quit! I don't want to live like this! But I do not know who I really am- or what I am supposed to be doing with my life! Run where? I'm just going to be a chameleon! I will survive by blending into my surroundings! Run Kasona! Run! Run! Run where? Everywhere I go someone hurts me! There is no safe place! I don't understand! Run Kasona! Run! Just keep going! You are going to make it!

> *Exercise*: Have you ever felt that you had nowhere to go or nowhere to turn? Y or N. If yes, what did you do? Using one word, describe how you felt when you read the Introduction.

Conflict/Family

In my mind, my family was like the Hatfield's and McCoy's, without the shootings, in the small town of Glenwood, Georgia. My mom's side of the family viewed my dad's side of the family as bad people. My dad's side of the family viewed my mother's side of the family as high-minded people. Thus, when I visited either side, one talked badly about the other as if I was not in the room. This caused me severe agony and pain because I am a Newkirk and I'm a Troup. Therefore, in my mind, I had no true family. This was the origin of Satan isolation tactic. This was him going for the main artery. Thus, it was here where I *fell through the cracks* because when I could not have my way with one side of the family, I would just go to the other side because they did not like one another.

This also led to feelings of rejection and isolation that I am sure later encouraged me to not be a part of a "click." Additionally, I always wanted to look just like my mother. To me, she was and still is the most beautiful woman that I have ever seen. From my child's lenses, she was light skinned complexion, long, beautiful black hair, and pearly white teeth. Oh, how I wanted to look like my mother! However, all I heard was "you look just like them Newkirk's." Let me insert right here that the Newkirk's are the most beautiful people that you would ever want to meet. Yet, from the child's lens, that bad seed that the Newkirk's were bad people had been planted. What happened? I could not see my beauty, so I started out with a complex seeing beauty in everyone else except myself. The Abuse that would come from my beauty and being *fine as wine*, though I could not see it then, **almost** destroyed me. One day I will make it! I will not live like this all my life! I just got to keep going somehow. Lord, help me, but I am angry at the Lord. How can I ask Him for help? Run Kasona run! Just keep running!

> **Note**: If you have experienced this (black sheep) in your family or know someone who has, just know that Jesus made you exactly how he intended, which is BEAUTIFUL. Don't give up because you may be angry with God. I assure you, that Jesus understands all things and He will not abandon you even if you are angry right now. He knows that one day you will come into the knowledge of the truth.
>
> *Exercise*: Read Revelations 12:7-17 (special focus on verse 12). Reflect on how this scripture is related to you.

Hopeless

In this isolation bullying and mental and physical abuse ran rampant. I know you are probably wondering when and who. I will say that it started around 7 years old. What is going on? I felt as though I was holding a sign that read "abuse me." Additionally, grown people introduced me to drugs and alcohol. I was sick, crying inside, but nobody could see it because all they could see were my symptoms. I abhorred these people from my inside, but I dare not show it. I hated the people that were slandering me. In my mind, they were stupid because they should have been helping instead of ridiculing me. I just had to survive!!! Run Kasona! Run! I did!

> **Note**: This book is about overcoming things that tried to kill me. Thus, I am revealing the name that needs to be revealed and that is the spirit of Satan. I am merely revealing the culprit because he is the one that needs to be revealed FIRST. The people that did the acts were overcome by the spirit of Satan. That is why it is important to pray for people because if it were not for Jesus, that spirit of Satan could overtake any one of us at any time. If this were not true, then Jesus would not have warned us in John 10:10 stating that the thief comes only to steal and kill and destroy.

If you are someone or you know someone that is currently experiencing mental or physical abuse, you must tell someone **that can do something about it**. I did not know this then, but the ENEMY is counting on you not to tell that one somebody that can help. Perhaps when you look around your immediate circle for help, there is none. That is where you must press to tell someone that can help outside your immediate circle. There is a difference between telling someone who can help and telling someone who will make matters worse for you. Now they have hotlines you can call to remain anonymous. You keep calling until you get some help. No one will have to know that it is you. Trust me, the abuse is not going to stop, it will only get bolder and bolder. That person that the enemy is using to destroy you is hoping that you will not tell. On the other hand, if you were mentally or physically abused in the past, then do the work to become wholesome within yourself by seeking a Mental Health Counselor and a Spiritual Guide, among other things. This book was written to share with you the things that I have done and continue to do as an act of Self-Care.

The bottom line is that we all know right from wrong. The bottom line is that we all have done things that we are not proud of, but sin has been graded. You cannot go back into the past. I had to stop blaming myself for what happened to me! Period! Sometimes people get lost in needing closure. This is certainly where I got stuck. The remedy for that is being in the knowledge of the truth and allowing that knowledge of the truth to set you free. Give yourself closure knowing that you are a child of God, and you have an assignment on your life to be a light in a dark world. Not only can you make a difference in others life, but you can make a difference in your OWN life. For that reason, the spirit of Satan has tried to and is still trying to kill God's children by any means necessary, using whomever he can to do so. There is not but one Man I know that can redeem you some time, and that is Jesus. Jesus redeemed time for me because I had wasted so much time in the past by making current decisions based off the past. *Point*: Start from where you are right now.

> *Exercise*: Read 2 Thessalonians 2:6-8. Reflect on what you read and what it means to you. Write in journal.

Junior High & High School

Kasona, please don't quit! I don't want to go to school like this! Kasona, what is wrong? Your grades are dropping. She needs to be moved out of A group and placed into a lower group. No! She doesn't need to be moved! Something is wrong with her! Kasona, what is wrong?

Kneeling on the ground, embracing me as only she could, Ms. Edna Terrell (a teacher and dear friend to my mother) compelled me not to quit school. Kasona, please don't quit school? Please! You are too smart! She convinced me not to quit. She took me to BC Moore's, a clothing store in McRae, Georgia, and purchased me some clothing. Oh Lord! I went on to school…ashamed, depressed…despondent.

The teacher that would not let the administration take me out of A group (Mr. Sandy Morrison) was heartbroken. It was confirmed that something was wrong with me after all. Before long, they had no choice but to take me out of the A group because my grades plummeted! I could not remember anything! I lost my mind, but I did not know it at the time. I was using a coping mechanism unbeknownst to me. I would push all the bad things out of my life. In doing so, I cannot recall many wonderful people and happy moments in my mind. I would go to sleep and try not to wake up, but wake up I did, and all

I could do was say the numbers and letters on my Winnie the Pooh curtains that hung from my windows to stay sane.

> **Note:** I did not know this then, but the way to deal with lies and shame is simply not to try to. I know that you want to be able to convey your side, but it doesn't matter because most people want to believe the worst. Therefore, don't say anything, just keep doing your best.
>
> **Question:** If you had a $100 dollar bill in your pocket and somebody was declaring that you did not have any money, especially $100, would you try to prove to them that you have that $100? Now, you can pull out your $100 if you choose to, but why should you? You know for certain that you have $100 dollars in your pocket. I am not saying that lies don't hurt because they certainly do! It is *how* we deal with it though. Thus, you must choose your battles. Is it worth it? Kasona, you will get through this if you just hold on! Hold on to what? I'm angry at Jesus! I don't know, just hold on. I tell myself that this is not your life.
>
> **Question:** In what ways do you currently deal with stress and depression? Picture in your mind other ways that you could deal with stress and depression.
>
> **Note:** I learned to pray and picture myself laying in Jesus' arms telling him about all my problems until I feel better.

Scripture: John 14: 1-2: Let not your heart be troubled: ye believe in God, believe also in me. In my Father's house are many mansions: if it were not so, I would have told you.

Basketball, Reading, and Me

Watch out for #10! If we can stop #10, we might have a chance to win the game! Basketball was one of my favorite hobbies that I used as an exit from this world. Nothing bothered me while I was playing basketball! My other escape was reading. I loved to read Dean R. Koontz novels. His writing was especially vivid, and it felt as though I was inserted in the storyline. For example, at one point, one of Koontz characters was in a cave. I could feel the heat, touch the wetness, and smell the odor that the cave possessed. Koontz was one of the many authors that I enjoyed. I read anything that would captivate my interest. It didn't matter what genre it was. It could be national geographic, the Bible, love novels, magazines. I just needed it for take-off! This catalyst propelled me into a different world.

Anyway, I graduated high school at the age of 17 years old. I thank God for my real-life superman at that time, Coach Ralph Hardy. He would take the time to have real life conversations with me. My most memorable moment of him was seeing him run across the campus coming to see about me after I had run the car into the ditch while trying to take my daughter to the babysitter who lives near the school. There were many occasions that he should have expelled me from school. Yet, he did not, and I'm so glad that he gave me opportunity after opportunity to get myself together. However, I had no idea of what I wanted to do with my life. Nonetheless, there are two things that I knew that I was not going to do and those are being piss poor, cleaning folk's houses for a couple of dollars and some fish out of their ponds! Nope!

> **Exercise:** Describe a time that you were shown an act of love when you didn't deserve it due to your attitude or behavior. Would you consider paying it forward? Write in journal.

College Round 1

I attended Brewton-Parker College on a basketball scholarship. I could not focus. There was hardly any food and no pretty clothes to wear to my classes. I was not accustomed to nobody in my face hollering and yelling about a play that we were not executing correctly. Plus, I had to take developmental courses first. What a bomber! None of the developmental courses were applied to my degree program. That is what happens sometimes when you are the star player in high school. I finally managed to be placed on academic probation. While attending school, I managed to work at Husqvarna for a short span. The job required assembling lawn mowers as they moved down an assembly line. The plant wreaked of oil smells! I quickly realized that assembly line work was not for me either. Uh oh! I got dismissed from Brewton-Parker for academic suspension! What was I to do? I just had to finish! Run! Run! Run Kasona! Don't give up now! You cannot quit now! At one of my lowest moments, Jesus allowed me to recall words that Mrs. Dorothy Hall spoke to my mom. Kasona is a fighter.

Exercise: Describe how you deal with setbacks.

Military Reserves

I know what I can do! I will go into the military so I can qualify for the GI Bill! Fort Jackson here I come! *Hey, hey Captain Jack.... meet me down by the railroad tracks.... with my weapon in my hand.... I'm going to be a fighting man....* It is amazing at how the drill sergeants could sing those cadences! Those cadences got us through miles of marching and running the hills of South Carolina and Virginia. Privates, why are you here? To live, to die, to fight for my country! Private why are you here? For the GI Bill Sir! Okay, I am looking around asking myself- what are you doing here? Survive Kasona! You cannot quit, I told myself! It was then that I thought about the weakest person that I know who completed basic training. I kept them in my forethoughts because I told myself if they can do it, then so can I.

Meanwhile, after all my training, I returned to my hometown of Glenwood, Georgia and later reported to my duty station in Dublin, Georgia. I got a job at the hospital as a respiratory therapy assistant, and I worked at a rural health care clinic filing Medicaid claims. I returned to school in the evenings at Brewton-Parker College. This time, I excelled! Yet, I am tired of my lifestyle outside of school. Two children, hardly any money, and constantly partying took their toll. I had a deep longing in my heart that to this day is indescribable. Miserable soul! Why was I so lonely. Snap out of it Kasona! You must! I can't even get high anymore! Sleep had deserted me! Snap out of it! Read a good book! I am trying, but nothing is working. I feel myself dying! Anxiety attacks too aggressive! Oh Lord, I am not ready! I'm not ready! I don't want to be playing church! My oldest child becomes sick unto death. What now?

Exercise: Write in your journal how you cope with unexpected life changes.

Note: If you are going through this, that is why the scripture tells us to come to Jesus just as we are. Yet, because of how we may have been raised, we thought that we had to get good and stop doing things. This is not true! It is a lie. Our loving Father does not care how dirty we are. Think about a baby and its parents. When the baby makes a mess or defecates on themselves, the parent(s) clean them up and throw the soiled items in the trashcan. However, they do not throw the baby away with the soiled materials. Indeed, the baby is not thrown away in the garbage with the clean up! This is how it really is with Jesus. He cleans His children up with His word and continues to love us.

The Turning Point

I walk into the hospital room with a mask on. My daughter's white blood cell count is 6. The doctors cannot find the cause of her condition. I could see and smell death on her. There are no words to explain what death looks and smells like, but you will recognize it if you ever meet it. I climbed into the hospital bed with my daughter until she fell asleep. Then, I fell to my knees and SINCERELY prayed. Lord, if you heal my daughter, I promise you that I will serve You and seek Your face. Here I am Lord, I will not continue to run from You any longer. By the end of the week, my daughter was released from the hospital with doctors in awe of her recovery because they still did not know the cause of her illness.

> **Note:** The Lord knows how to get our attention. Sometimes He will do things to get us to seek Him. Ultimately, I still had a choice. I could have chosen to continue the way I was going, even after He healed my daughter. Yet, I had made Him a vow. Thus, I appreciated Him for loving me enough to get my attention to turn to Him. Nobody knows, but me, where I was headed. I was headed for destruction. I truly understand that the path that I was following would have certainly led me to my death. For example, if a toddler picks up a knife playing with it, the parent(s) will rush to get the knife

out of the toddler's hands since they know that the knife would more than likely bring the child harm or even death. God chose to take the knife out of my hands in His own way.

Entering the Cocoon

I was struggling, but I was still not the same. I searched high and low. I went back to the church (Starlight) that I grew up in as a child. I went to the alter as the preacher did the alter call and I gave the Pastor my hand. He directed me to sit in the sister's corner. If you are facing the pulpit, the sister's corner is on the right side. I went over and sat with the older females that made up the sister's corner, but something was missing. I still had a deep longing in my soul. Therefore, I stood up and returned to the seating area where the rest of the congregation were seated with tears in my eyes and with a bowed down head. I didn't know what to think except that I couldn't be saved because I was too bad. From there I continued to seek God at other assemblies such as Methodists, Holiness, Catholics, and television Preachers. After much searching, I became despondent because I felt that there was no help for me. One night, I lay on the floor in the backroom of my grandmother's house crying. Lord, if you are real, save me! I moaned and groaned to Him for I felt as though I did not have the words to touch Him. I cannot take another step Lord! I am going to die! Lord, do You care if I die? Lord, if you are real, please help me! Like a whirlwind, His presence began to fill my room and I could see halos in the air. He did not speak to me, but I knew that it was Him. He had given me Hope.

Shortly after that experience, I started to wonder about who I could talk to about my experience. I thought about my Aunt Sarah, a devout Christian woman. I remembered how she never judged me when I was around her. She always gave me encouraging words. I started to remember how I used to go to her farm as a little girl with my grandfather (her brother) and play with the animals. You see prior to this experience the devil had my mind, and he would not let me think about this great woman of God though she was accessible to me. All the devil would allow me to think about my Aunt Sarah was that she did not celebrate Christmas and the rest of the holidays. I remembered how transparent she was about her own life experiences in our conversations. I picked up the phone and I called my Aunt Sarah. We talked into the "wee" hours of the morning. She comforted me like a mother hen comforts her chicks as I told her that I felt as though I was too bad for the Lord to save me.

Aunt Sarah travailed in prayer and sang songs to me over the phone assuring me that Jesus loved me and could save me. I went to visit her the next day and she gave me a book to read entitled The Memoir of the Apostle Reverend W.J. Peterson by Mother Jennell Peterson Faison. Oh my God! As I read the book, the words gripped my soul stronger than Koontz's novels and I wept uncontrollably. Finally, I had so many questions answered for the first time! Later, Aunt Sarah gave me cassette tapes to listen to. These tapes were preaching messages from Bishop William Duren, Bishop Eugene Rice, Bishop C.L. Rawls, and Bishop J.J. Sears of The Pentecostal Church of God. As I lie in bed listening to the messages through my headphones, I could feel something like electricity going through my body! I did not know it then, but it was LIFE! Real Life!

Later, Aunt Sarah invited me to church, but I felt that I was alright now, so I just allowed my children to go with her. Eventually, I decided to go with her to The Pentecostal Church of God, Newnan Georgia assembly. She explained to me that this was a special fourth Sunday meeting that Bishop Eugene Rice would be preaching in. As I walked through the doors, a weight was released off my shoulders! I whispered a sigh of relief that only I could hear, "I am home." The service had not started yet as the usher ushered me to my seat. Next, a man named Elder Lee Frazier came into the pulpit to lead the devotional part of the service. After many songs of praises, he began to lead the prayer. I had never heard anyone pray like this, and I was moved within myself to say, "yes Lord." I began to be Godly sorry for my sins. I thought that my heart would completely burst open!

As I lifted my head from the prayer, I saw Bishop Eugene Rice enter the pulpit and he began to preach. As he spoke, he talked about things that I had done and what I was currently experiencing. I knew that I had not spoken about these things to anyone. I knew that this was God talking through him. Before I realized it, I was standing in the aisle, so close to the podium at the edge of the pulpit that I could touch it. People all around me had their hands in the air, but I was new, and I felt that I did not want people to see me reach out. Even though I was not stretching forth my hands, I was stretching forth my heart. Within, I was saying Lord, if I could just touch the hem or your garment, I would be alright. He allowed me to touch the hem of his garment. Jesus granted me that Spirit of Repentance through His word as Bishop Eugene Rice preached it. The Lord permitted my children and I to be baptized that day when Bishop Rice opened the door for God's children to come home.

> **Note:** When the Lord calls you, you cannot help but to move. You will have no control over it, and you will not be satisfied with anything in life until you come. It is a movement from within your soul and is desiring to return to the Creator. No matter how embarrassed you may feel, it is okay. Trust me, the people standing around are probably in a worser shape than you are. When you realize that you will drown if you do not move, people around you just want matter. The matter is between you and God.

> **Exercise:** Reflect on Proverbs 3:3. Write in your journal.

Inside the Cocoon

I returned home and continued with life. I started attending the local Pentecostal Church of God at the Lumber City, Georgia assembly. Habits and an old acquaintance reared its ugly head! I fell into the trap, but it didn't have the same effect on me. Another great thing happened. My mother and I had always had a strained relationship from all the family conflict. One night as I lay in bed it began to rain heavily, and out of nowhere tears rolled down my cheeks as I thought about my mother. She had visited my grandmother earlier that day and was telling my grandmother how bad her head was hurting. The Lord allowed me to recall that conversation. This is important because prior to this moment, I was numb to my mother. It was well after midnight during this conviction of my heart. I could not and did not want to wait until the next day to visit my mother. I drove to her house in the storm. Even though she only lived 7 miles away, I could not get there fast enough. I rang her doorbell and when she opened the door, I fell into her arms sobbing, telling her how sorry I was for taking her through so many changes!

Additionally, the Lord, through His word, convinced my heart about forgiving my daddy, I slowly began the process. Bishop Rice explained to me that I would not make it into God's Kingdom with the hate I felt in my heart towards my dad. Bishop continued to provide away for me to get over it. He told me to think about one good thing that my daddy had ever done for me and meditate and be thankful about that one thing. After much reluctance, my heart did begin to change. I started to think about how he used to take me fishing, hunting, allowed me to drive his boat on the river, and he cosigned for me a candy apple red Grand Am car. Another major credit that I give my dad is that he did try to get all of his children together.

In fact, in my very early years, I could eat the ground my daddy walked on. However, after his abusive ways towards us, I hated him. I hated that he told me that my mother didn't love me. I hated that he took me to all his women's houses. I hated that he had all these other children from other women, whose children referred to me as their half-sister or stepsister. This Gospel, that I had been exposed to would eventually answer that very burning question about a stepsister. I learned that since it is the man that discharges the seed, it makes my siblings and I whole brothers and sisters, not half. I hated him for taking care of other women children instead of his own. Yet, because Jesus gave me grace and mercy to hearken to His voice and humble myself, Jesus helped me to remember some happy moments with my daddy. The truth is no parent is without fault and now I truly love my dad as if none of this ever happend. Maybe he was doing all he knew to do. The miracle begins when Jesus gives you a heart of flesh to pray for sight for the person that has caused so much pain

I needed a change. I needed to move away from Glenwood, Georgia. There was absolutely nothing to do in this small town. To me, it was desolate and depressing, so I moved to Newnan,

Georgia with my cousin Millicent (Aunt Sarah's daughter). I made a lot of mistakes here being a babe in Christ, still feeling uncomfortable and vulnerable, not knowing what I was going to do or how I was going to work. In fact, I did not have a job yet. I should have been more helpful to my cousin, but I was so wrapped up in myself (selfish). Later, I moved to Atlanta, Georgia with my cousin Kenneth to hopefully get a better job. Kenneth doesn't understand the change that has taken place in my life. We were all once party animals! They used to call us the A-team because Kenneth owned a black box van that resembled the van on the hit television series called the A-Team featuring Mr. T. Kenneth was nice enough to allow me to stay with him. However, I almost burned his apartment up cooking gizzards one day. As if that was not enough, I returned home to get my children against Kenneth's will. Nevertheless, my children and I became homeless. We lived in the car and in hotels until I finally could move into an apartment in Decatur, Georgia with the help of the church.

> **Note:** Sometimes in transition, when you are becoming a new person, you will make many mistakes. If someone allows you to live with them, do what you can to make their load lighter such as cook and clean the house. I know that you feel as though you are drowning, and you hate that you are so dependent on others, but you must make the best of the situation by being as helpful and grateful as you possibly can. I know that it is new and uncomfortable, but you can do it. Try to think of the person that you are staying with needs and do what is in your power to do. You may not be able to give them any money, but do what you can. It is the small things

that you can do to show a token of appreciation. I thank God for my cousins Millicent and Kenneth for allowing me to live with them. I honestly do not know how they put up with me for as long as they did. God must have taught their hearts because it was not anything good that I did.

Exercise: How to deal with starting over. Write a plan.

My children and I started going to the Pentecostal Church of God, Newnan, Georgia assembly. We did not know anybody there but my cousins Millicent and her brother Larry. There is a huge age gap between us, so even though we are related, the kids and I don't really know them. We began to really walk through the fire as we had some church members treat us horribly. On many occasions, I wanted to return home to Glenwood, but after much thought, I realized that I had already tried Glenwood. There was nothing there but my old way of life. I had to try and endure the hardships. I recall sharing what my kids and I were going through with some of the church members to Bishop Rico. He told me something that shocked me. He explained that I thought that I had a testimony prior to coming to the church, but that I really didn't. He continued to explain that the trials and tribulations that I would have to go through in the church would give me a testimony. He explained that I had to be made over again. It is important to note that he did not condone the actions of some of the members, but he had to tell me the truth. There are some people in and around the church that are not going to be saved. Then sometimes God allow things to happen to his children.

Exercise: Write in journal discussing how you can try to be friendly to others when you are hurting.

In hindsight, I did not understand what he meant, but today, I can say that I truly understand. He also told me that there are some people in the church that really and truly loved the Lord and my children and me. He was certainly telling the truth. However, the pain was so great coming from the ones that didn't love us, that we could not focus on the people that did. My children were going through triple trouble because they still had to endure a young mother that was a baby in the Lord who had had so much taken from her. I had endured so much that I did not have anything to give them. There were days that I did not even cook after I got off work because I would go into my room, close the door wondering if I could pay the bills. Again, caught up in self. Yet, we trudged forward the best we could. Run! Run Kasona run! You have got to make it!

Watch out! Yes, another roadblock! I did not want to continue living from check to check, or shall I say robbing Peter to pay Paul because there was never enough money to pay bills. I knew that I had to return to school. The problem was that I still owed Brewton-Parker College because the GI Bill did not cover my college cost 100%, and they would not release my transcripts without full payment. Therefore, I relied on other avenues to get an education. The "Word" had taught me that where there is a will, that there is a way. I utilized the WIA program through Fulton County to get funding for school. While the program did not put any money in my pocket, it did pay the school the full one hundred percent for me to attend.

Additionally, WIA only paid for short-term programs, not for degrees. Under WIA, I gained certifications as a Medical Assistant and Nail Care Specialist. I was personally able to pay for training to become a certified Personal Fitness Trainer and Reflexologist. Unfortunately, my children would have to endure more suffering because I was never at home. As soon as my daughter graduated from the Christian Academy, she ran away from home with her boyfriend and father of my four beautiful grandchildren. This was too much for me to bear. I was at one of my all-time lowest points. I stayed in Atlanta a few more years, until I reached my final breaking point.

I drove myself to the cemetery and asked the Lord to let me die. He did not and I contemplated suicide. I decided that I would move to West Palm Beach Florida with my cousin Darlene. I remember calling my mother on the phone, not able to talk for crying. What she did was miraculous. She started singing to me until I was able to get myself together. I packed just a few things and left Atlanta deciding not to go to Florida. Instead, I decided to take care of my grandmother who was now ill. I had expressed my love to my grandmother and told her that she would not have to go to a nursing home. The Lord allowed me to honor my word to her. After almost 20 years of living in Atlanta, I returned to Glenwood. The three-hour drive back to Glenwood was excruciating. I thought my whole world was over. During the entire drive all I could moan over and over was Jesus, I love you and I love our great leaders.

> **Exercise:** Prioritize what most important to you in your life right now.

When I returned to Glenwood, I was done with church folks. Not only was I broken spiritually but naturally also. There was a pain in my chest that would not leave. I asked the Lord why? Why did this happen to us since I was following Him? After much agony, He gave me an answer. His answer was, Why not You? Just as you would watch your favorite television show, Jesus showed the Why of the death of His Son to me. He showed me what His Son went through for me, and He loved His only begotten son. He showed me how His son had to suffer. He showed me that I was blessed and highly favored to have suffered in this manner.

Though he revealed all this to me, I still decided that I did not want any part of church. However, Jesus would not let me rest. For He had a job for me to do, but I did not know it yet. He never let me be content in whatever I tried. I found myself many nights sleeping on my knees justifying my actions. I eventually started going to all different denominations of churches, but I did not and could not fit in. Every time the preacher would get up before the congregation, the message was gone back.

One day I received a call from Bishop Frankie Key of The Pentecostal Church of God. When I heard his voice, my heart melted for he and his wife had given me much support during my stay in Atlanta. I told him that I was sick and had lost a lot of weight. He asked me why I had not called him, and I explained to him that I knew that he would tell me that I needed to be in church. I just didn't want to hear that at the time. To my surprise, he began to cry. Bishop Key assured me that he would not ask me to come to church, he just wanted to hear from me occasionally. Before we ended our conversation, he told me that he knew that I was God's daughter and promised that I would be okay. After that conversation, I went back to The Pentecostal Church of God in Lumber City, Georgia.

> **Note:** Sometimes we focus on the many things that are tormenting us instead of on the prize. There were people in the Pentecostal Church of God that loved my children and me. They were genuinely concerned for our well-being. That call from Bishop Frankie Key reminded me of that. I began to see the people in the church that had shown us so much love. I repented in my heart and that pain in my chest was gone. If you have left the church because of people, just know that that pain came from some of the people, but not all of people. Some of the people love you more than you will ever know, but the enemy will not let you see them and embrace their love. He causes you to focus on the negative. Readjust your focus if you can. I must say that I learned that even that is a favor from the Lord. Also, ask yourself do you really love Jesus. If you really love Jesus, then you will serve Him. Your faithfulness to the church will not be about the people, but your Love for Jesus. If you love God, then serve Him in the midst of them.
>
> **Exercise:** Write in Journal. What does forgiveness do to the forgiver.

I'm not out of the woods yet. Another trap is coming. Another seducing spirit would entangle me again to try and take my life. I marry a worldly man from Dublin. In my mind, I tell myself that he is older, settled, and seems to love the Lord. You see, the enemy will put out his bait and he will play around with you until you get hooked. Once you get hooked, he tries with all his might to kill you. You see, he is not playing with us. He salivates after God's children. This house was like a haunted house. You see Jesus had something else for me. I vividly recall seeing my true husband as I stood in my kitchen washing dishes in Dublin. I said to myself, he is married, and I am married. I dismissed it but could never shake it. Anyway, the Lord had to make it unbearable for me to leave Dublin. He literally ripped me out of the enemies' hands by using His word during a church convention in Winter Haven Florida. That gave me the courage to say Lord, I am willing to walk away if you give me a way for me to escape. Jesus did. I had lost so much and had wasted so much time. I went to a meeting in Virginia. In that meeting, the Lord redeemed the time for me. My Lord, Jesus is the only one that can redeem time.

Coming out the Cocoon

While driving home from work one evening, I had a car accident. The Lord allowed me to have this accident so that I would not have any distractions. I began to get counseling from Bishop James Stoudemire. I talked to Bishop often, but my heart was still somewhat hard. In one of our conversations, he said something that only the Lord knew, for I had not told him. He proceeded to say that if I wanted what the Lord had for me, that I had to stop living in the past. He told me that I had to get up. I asked him to put me in his pocket, and I earnestly began to pray for help. I started to get better, and the enemy would come again. At the time, I was living in Warner Robins, Georgia known for its Air Force Base. I had many pursuers. Yet, I told the Lord, I wanted to wait.

I am not telling you that this was easy. It was not easy. For about 3 years, I would not be in a relationship. Right when I was about to give up, the Lord sent my now husband. The same man that I saw at my kitchen sink while I washed dishes in Dublin. Out of the blue he came back into my life and from that point, we did not want to be apart. He is an honorable man of God. He loves Jesus. He loves God's people. I do not claim that He is perfect, for neither am I. Jesus is our glue, and He holds us together through our trials and tribulations. Most importantly, the Lord allows us to work together in His service. All of this and more that the Lord has done.

I had to go through. I had to go through. When Jesus has a call on your life, you will go through. Yes, I am still going through. I would not take anything for my journey now. It has caused me to Love Jesus more. Jesus had to break me and make me over again. It probably hurt him to have to break me, but it was for my good. I thank Him so much for loving me enough to hurt me, to make me better.

I pray that as you have read this book, that your heart was captivated as my heart was when I read the book on the Apostle Reverend W.J. Peterson. He was the man that laid the foundation for The Pentecostal Church of God. This book was not written for pity, but as a demonstration on the Power of Jesus Christ. My real life HERO. It was written as a guide to hopefully let others know that somebody else went through horrific things too and help others to come out on the other side triumphantly spiritually and naturally. Amen.

The Point is when you TRULY want to better yourself, there are going to be challenges and obstacles. There will be indescribable resistances. Maybe you want to be a better person in general. Maybe you want to be a better mother. Maybe you want a certificate in say welding. Maybe you want to be an LPN. Maybe you just want to get out of bed. May you want to just leave the house. Maybe you want to be a realtor. Maybe you want to be a Dentist. Maybe you want a Doctoral Degree. Whatever it is that you want, you must make the sacrifice.

It all boils down to denying yourself the life your friends around you are having for a season. In all honesty, you will find that once you get what you are seeking, you will not be comfortable with the old way of thinking because now you have pushed yourself and made great strides. You have realized what it takes for you to get to where you want to be. This is your journey and yours alone. You will find that you will want to keep expanding, keep growing. The bottom line is that the MIND has to change.

I dare not say none of my achievements spiritually or naturally have been easy. All the sleepless nights, going to McDonald's parking lot in the middle of the night trying to use their WIFI to get an assignment turned in when my cable was turned off. Being on road trips and having people take you to a hotel lobby to use their WIFI to turn in an assignment. Trying to work but can hardly function due to sleep deprivation. Having anxiety attacks or nervous breakdowns daily and weekly. Yet through it all, I got mine. I sought God's world FIRST, and then He allowed me to achieve my Doctorate Degree in this world that I might share my knowledge and wisdom with others.

In closing, currently I am a wife, a mother, a doting grandmother, and a praying woman. I have many certificates and degrees, but the one degree that I am most proud of is my BA (Born Again). I am providing a first-class Christian education to students of all ages, but in particular to students diagnosed with Specific Learning Disorders (SLD) in reading. For more information on how to work with me, please visit coatesacademy.org. Thank you and may God richly bless you.

A Letter to Dr. Coates

In our experience, now and then, you will meet teachers. They come and go. They teach material well. They know how to direct students, and lead them to personal victories through tests and well planned lessons. They wear the badge well, motivating academic success and inspiring pupils all the while appearing to be stress free or unaffected by the chaos that comes daily on the road to educate. This is the path they have chosen……

…..A Good Path.

Some of these skills they learned from other teachers. While others stem from their intense desire to advance others, Combined with the uniqueness to focus on accomplishing a goal. They love to encourage others and see them grow……

…….It's a Good Cause

Impactful but human, eventually flaws show. In the heat of that daily stress of teaching, they somehow drop the ball. They lose the faith of a student, maybe a few. They lose their cool and damage the trust that they have built. They had a bad day, and it showed out. What can you say? It's part of life, I'm human after all. Regardless, they get back up, dust off and carry on. Back on task they keep teaching, understanding the value of moving on from mistakes……

.......they fight a good fight.......

……...proving to be a good teacher…..

Now, if you are lucky, you will meet a teacher that is something more. A person who is divinely set in your path. A genuine friend. A masterful mentor. Consistent with the type of love that is a steady comfort. They are built upon the Rock☩

…….Something Special.

You will swear this teacher is an angel. Touching every life she encounters, her parenting quality adopts you, her presence comforts you. She builds you up. She listens to you and sees where you are fragile, somehow soothes you and helps you become strong again. She proves in her actions superior devotion far above the norm. Always strong, never breaking your trust, always honest, always teaching…

……she changes your life.

Knowing exactly when to push and when to back off, she helps you grow. Seeing you not only for who you are, never what you were, but who you are meant to be, all while making sure you see it too. She in-spires lasting change.

Never the judge, always the support. She unites you with peers and calls you the dream team…………..

…..then sets off to fly. What you have to understand is that teachers like this have to move on, they are under heavenly assignment. But when they leave, they leave you with the confidence and motivation to strive for greatness in your own life…..

……A lesson that lasts a life time. This teacher was more than good. She was an angel, a miracle woman, that once in a life time type of blessing…...

……Dr. Coates this teacher was you. Thank you so much for every day you have spent with us. You truly made a difference in my quality of life. You helped me through a very tender time……you never once put the blame of my sufferings on to me; although, they are my fault. You treated me like a man who has been redeemed. You showed Christ in your every action and it changed my life to know you. I'll never stop what you have started, I'll teach forever now.

Thank you to you and your family. God bless you all! What you have done in our lives we could never express. We will not forget you and we will make you proud!

We love you Dr. Coates.

Your students and teaching assistants

A Poem for YOU
(by Hermeione Flowers)

Metamorphosis: Why Not Me

One day long time ago
As I stood in Winter Waters
I heard the voice of God
Speaking to His dear daughter

It was through the Men of God
That I heard His great voice
He wanted to make me better
For of me, He had made a choice

I wondered where to start
I really did not know
But it was one trial at a time
While dwelling in the Overflow

I desired that great change
That the natural eye could not see
For what the natural eye doth see
Is really not the real me

Years and years of trials
And seasonal torrential rains
Altered my path of destruction

And made beauty from the pain

When I kneeled before Jesus Christ
My heart was lifted high
It was all I had to offer Him
I asked Him to OCCUPY…MY..🖤

Do not seek to outrun
The change God has for you
Instead answer "Why Not Me"
For God knows your true value

Metamorphosis? Why Not Me?
I seek for spiritual progress
All to the Glory of God
His name I will always bless

Written in The Love of Jesus Christ

More Poems by Ms. Hermeione Flowers on Amazon

The Son Did Rise
Jesus is Lord
When I Am Gone
O' Precious Jesus Christ
The Power of Love
Jesus Loves Me
Pretty and Handsome Souls A Spiritual Fashion Show

Please visit Amazon.com: Search Hermeione Flowers
Contact Information: gillhermeione1107@gmail.com

Especially for the MAN

What should I do? Who can I talk to? Those are the questions that run through my head. I wish people understood me. Why do people feel like I got it all together? — because you're "a man"… you're supposed to have everything taken care of, right? This is a trap. Society teaches us that Men are supposed to do this or do that.. we are the stronger vessel but that doesn't mean we don't have needs. How do we confess our needs without being judged? Well, I believe that truly being a man means not caring what people think about you. Being vulnerable and open about what's going on in your life is not a sign of weakness. It's a sign of emotional intelligence. It's quite dumb or insane to suffer and pretend that there's nothing wrong. Unfortunately, that's how most of us handle situations. We have to learn how to be honest. Tell the truth on self. Being real with yourself is being a man. Being honest with God is being a man. Pretending is not like God.

The "Implementation" of the Word of God in my "real life" is my only concern, not what people think. I had to learn that Church life and real life should be the same, but it's not. Church life can be very religious. Religion isn't like Christ. So, pay more attention to how you're using the Word of God in your everyday life.. don't come to church to listen and then go home creating chaos and stress.

BEING A MAN of GOD

Church is a place where we are "supposed" to get strength and help. The Word of God is truly a healer if we use it right. But most of us don't know how to implement the Word of God in our lives, we just memorize it. I used to sit in church and battle with how I see things or how I feel, etc. I felt wrong within myself that I had mental struggles. Sometimes it's hard to admit to yourself that you have a problem. But nevertheless, if we proclaim to have God's spirit, then we will tell the truth. Most of us don't believe in God, we believe in "church".. but Church doesn't heal you, the Word of God does. If we all see God as a helper, then He'll help.. but if we don't tell him exactly what's going on and be ready to "PUT IN THE WORK TO CHANGE" then we'll forever be saying "AMEN" without the Word of God taking effect. Faith without works is dead. You have to work on yourself. The Holy Ghost doesn't do it for us.. We have to repent.. we have to change. We have to learn to tell the truth and communicate.. we have to learn how to be vulnerable without caring about what people think. We tell ourselves, "I got the word, I'll be alright." Yes, we do have the word, but what are we going to do with it? Most of us mistreat ourselves because we have accepted bad treatment from others. Sometimes "Church" can be a place you'll get hurt the most.. Most of us are even scared to admit that. But part of being a man is admitting the truth. Why lie or pretend like it's all good?

To all men, be real with God and with yourself. This one step alone will alleviate a lot of stress, depression, anxiety, and other Mental Illnesses. The truth shall set you free.

WORK ON YOURSELF. START WITH HONESTY and SELF-LOVE.

How To Start with Honesty and Self-Love

1. Pray and ask the Lord every day to show you yourself and how to be honest. This is how to lean on Him for strength to do the things we are too weak to do for ourselves.

2. Write down the things you need to change. This helps you to see yourself and put things in perspective.

3. Practice telling the truth. Forgive yourself by telling on yourself to the Lord for the small things first and work your way up to the hard things to admit. This is a form of repentance, but it's you taking real steps towards improvement. Not just praying and sobbing about it.

4. Apologize to the people you hurt. If they don't forgive you, don't take it personal. It's not on you anymore. You've done your part by apologizing and seeing your mistakes.

5. Admit that you're hurt to the people who hurt you. Forgive them. This is how you "Implement" the Word of God with self-love. Self-Love is showing God's love to yourself so you can show it to others.

Sometimes you may need professional help too. If that's the case, be honest with yourself about it. It's not a bad thing. Try to look at it the same as going to the doctor for physical pain. It's normal to seek clarity for your Mental Health. Mental Health is Spiritual Health. So, if you're a "MAN of GOD", you'll be concerned about your Spiritual Health. Your Spiritual Health is more than about church. Some of us have real issues that cause us to have the wrong spirit because our minds aren't healthy. If we get our Mental Health in a better state, then we will more than likely have a more peaceful spirit.

Thank you for listening. I wrote this with God's love and from some of my experiences. I'm 28 years old. That's young but age is just a number when it comes to the spirit.

To Continue to Work and See what Mr. John Bess has to offer please visit.

Visionary | Mindset Enthusiast | ½ Podcaster of @weinvestdifferentpod

https://linktr.ee/MrJohnMicahBess?utmsource=linktreeprofileshare&ltsid=4efc8e6d-e274-49cb-ad56-934bcb949296

@financialfashionnetwork

@bless_energy1

Watering YOUR Garden: 7 Day Activity Book

Note: Everyday find a "happy place" where you are dwelling where you can pray and meditate. (For example, my "happy place" is in the shower).

Day 1:

- Scripture - This I recall to my mind, therefore have I hope. It is of the Lord's mercies that we are not consumed, because his compassions fail not. They are new every morning: great is thy faithfulness. The Lord is my portion, saith my soul; therefore will I hope in him. The Lord is good unto them that wait for him, to the soul that seeketh him (Lamentations 3:21-25).
- Meditation (Minimum 10 min.) – 1st five minutes (only give thanks); 2nd five minutes (ask Jesus for what you need).
  - ☐ Self-love Act- Hug yourself real tight. Call your name and tell yourself you love you. (For example, Kasona, I love you; but most of all God loves you).
  - ☐ Listen to Song while dressing: Youtube-Chain Breaker by Zach Williams (Live from Harding Prison)
  - ☐ Lunch Break: Youtube 10 Minute Motivational Video- The Most Eye Opening Videos Ever by Motivation Ark
  - ☐ Worksheet: Self Awareness Assessment
  - ☐ Bedtime Scripture: When thou liest down, thou shalt not be afraid: yea, thou shalt lie down, and thy sleep shall be sweet (Proverbs 3:24).
  - ☐ Positive Quote: Jesus makes everything alright. (Bishop James Stoudemire)

WATERING YOUR GARDEN: 7 DAY ACTIVITY BOOK

SELF-AWARENESS
ASSESSMENT

READ THE PROMTS BELOW AND THINK ABOUT THE FIRST THING THAT COMES TO MIND. FILL YOUR ANSWERS OUT IN THE BLANK BOXES.

I AM A HUMAN BEING THAT...

LOVES	
WANTS TO	
IS DRIVEN BY	
IS INSPIRED BY	
HAS A HABIT OF	
IS HAPPIEST WHEN	
BELIEVES IN	
WOULD GIVE	
WILL ONE DAY	
HAS THE GOAL OF	
WHO NOTICES	
IS AFRAID OF	

Day 2:

- Scripture- For I know the thoughts that I think toward you, saith the Lord, thoughts of peace, and not of evil, to give you an expected end.
- Meditation (Minimum 10 min.)- 1st five minutes (only give thanks); 2nd five minutes (ask Jesus for what you need).
- Self-love Act- Hug yourself real tight. Call your name and tell yourself you love you. (For example, Kasona, I love you; but most of all God loves you).
- Listen to Song while dressing: What are You Waiting For by Shawn McDonald
- Lunch Break: YouTube 10 Minute Motivational Video-10 Minutes for the Next 10 years- Denzel Washington Motivational Speech by Motivation2Study
- Worksheet: Journaling Challenge Bingo
- Bedtime Scripture: For God hath not given us the spirit of fear; but of power, and of love, and of a sound mind.
- Positive Quote: Where there is a will, there is a way (Bishop Eugene Rice).

WATERING YOUR GARDEN: 7 DAY ACTIVITY BOOK

Journaling Challenge Bingo

How am I feeling today?	The person I admire the most are ... because ...	Things I'm gratefull for in 2023	The best advice I ever get is ...	Write a love letter to myself
What do I love most about my body? Why?	1 year from now, I will be ...	My biggest fear is ...	Do I believe in luck?	What are the things I want the most in life?
My unforgettable memory would be ...	My favorite books are ...	Journaling Challengge	5 countries I want to visit are ...	Mu current bucket list is ...
How do I wish people to see me?	I can't stand people who are ...	Things that make me super happy are ...	The most special present I ever get was ... because ...	My favorite quote is ...
30 facts about myself are ...	10 songs that I love right now are ...	5 things that melt my heart would be ...	Let's talk about my first love	Something that I really miss is ...

www.reallygreatsite.com

Day 3:

- ☐ Scripture- But they that wait upon the Lord shall renew their strength; they shall mount up with wings as eagles; they shall run, and not be weary; and they shall walk, and not faint (Isaiah 40:31).
- ☐ Meditation (Minimum 10 min.)- 1st five minutes (only give thanks); 2nd five minutes (ask Jesus for what you need)
- ☐ Self-love Act- Hug yourself real tight. Call your name and tell yourself you love you. (For example, Kasona, I love you; but most of all God loves you).
- ☐ Listen to Song while dressing: Youtube- He'll Make It Alright by The P.C.G. Five
- ☐ Lunchbreak: Youtube 10 Minute Motivational Video- The Most Eye Opening 10 Minutes of Your Life with Simon Sinek by Motivation Ark
- ☐ Worksheet: 5 Finger Breathing: Mindful Coloring Mindful Positive Quote-I Can Do This.
- ☐ Bedtime Scripture: He will not let your foot slip- he who watches over you will not slumber (Psalms 121:3).
- ☐ Positive Quote: Lord, don't let me "tap" out no matter how hard it gets, help me to continue to say, Lord, I believe you! (Bishop Charles Wilson)

WATERING YOUR GARDEN: 7 DAY ACTIVITY BOOK

CALM YOURSELF WITH A
5 FINGER BREATHING
BRAIN BREAK

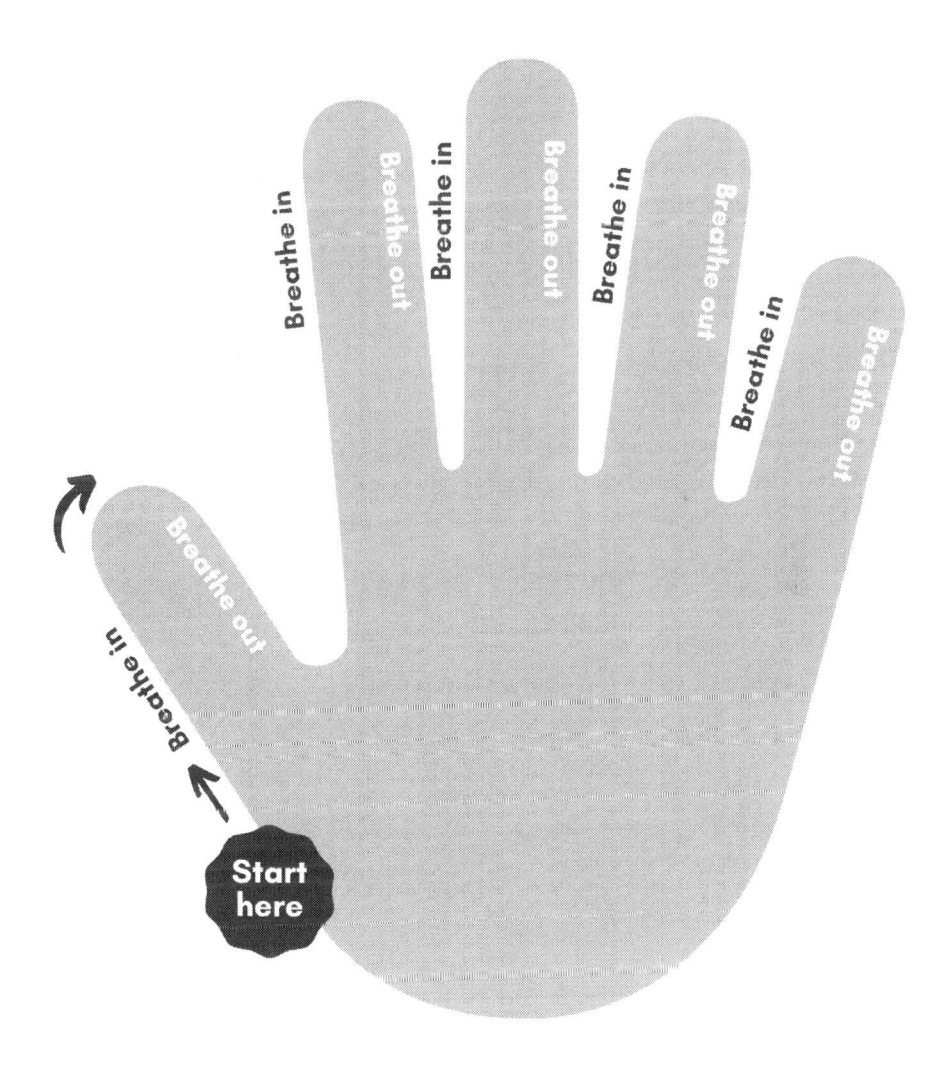

Breathe in · *Breathe out* · *Breathe in* · *Breathe out* · *Breathe in* · *Breathe out* · *Breathe in* · *Breathe out* · *Breathe in* · *Breathe out*

Start here

Slowly trace the outside of the hand with the index finger, breathing in when you trace up a finger and breathing out when you trace down. You can also do this breathing exercise using your own hand.

Day 4:

- **Scripture:-** By his power God raised the Lord from the dead, and he will raise us also (1 Corinthians 6:14).
- Meditation (Minimum 10 min.)- 1st five minutes (only give thanks); 2nd five minutes (ask Jesus for what you need)
- Self-love Act- Hug yourself real tight. Call your name and tell yourself you love you. (For example, Kasona, I love you; but most of all God loves you).
- Listen to Song while dressing: Youtube- Fight Song by Rachel Platten
- Lunchbreak: Youtube 10 Minute Video- 10 Minutes For the Next 10 Years of Your Life! Positive Morning Motivation to Listen Every Day by Motiversity
- Worksheet: Action Brainstorming-Minimal Action Brainstorm Goal Planning Worksheet
- Bedtime Scripture: Do not be anxious about anything, but in every situation, by prayer and petition, with thanksgiving, present your requests to God. And the peace of God, which transcends all understanding, will guard your hearts and your minds in Christ Jesus (Phillipians 4:6-7).
- Positive Quote: Jesus never Fails (Bishop William Duren).

ACTION
BRAINSTORMING

ACTION BRAINSTORMING CAN HELP IDENTIFY WHAT THINGS ARE HELPING OR STOPPING YOU FROM ACHIEVING YOUR GOALS.

MY GOAL:

STOP
DOING

DO
LESS OF

KEEP
DOING

DO
MORE OF

START
DOING

Day 5:

- Scripture: Therefore we do not lose heart. Though outwardly we are wasting away, yet inwardly we are being renewed day by day. For our light and momentary troubles are achieving for us an eternal glory that far outweighs them all. So we fix our eyes not on what is seen, but on what is unseen, since what is seen is temporary, but what is unseen is eternal (2 Corinthians 4:16-18).
- Meditation (Minimum 10 min.)- 1st five minutes (only give thanks); 2nd five minutes (ask Jesus for what you need)
- Self-love Act- Hug yourself real tight. Call your name and tell yourself you love you. (For example, Kasona, I love you; but most of all God loves you).
- Listen to Song while dressing: Youtube- I Won't Let You Fall by Hellen Miller
- Lunch break: Youtube 10 Minute- 10 Minutes to Start Your Day Right! Inspirational & Motivational Video by Motivation Ark
- Worksheet: Self-Care Assessment Planner
- Bedtime Scripture: Humble yourselves therefore under the mighty hand of God, that he may exalt you in due time: Casting all your care upon him; for he careth for you (1 Peter 5: 6-7).
- Positive Quote: It's not what it looks like (Bishop Andrew Stephens)

WATERING YOUR GARDEN: 7 DAY ACTIVITY BOOK

(Daily)
SELF-CARE

DATE ___ / ___ / ___

S M T W T F S

CHECKLIST

- ○ MAKE YOUR BED
- ○ TAKE YOUR MEDICATIONS & VITAMINS
- ○ SKINCARE ROUTINE
- ○ HEALTHY MEALS
- ○ GO FOR A WALK
- ○ CLEANING HOUSE
- ○ WASHING CLOTHES
- ○ LISTEN TO MUSIC
- ○ HAVE A POWER NAP
- ○ SOCIAL MEDIA BREAK

- ○ TAKE A LONG BATH
- ○ DO A FACE MASK
- ○ CALL A FRIEND OR FAMILY
- ○ MEDITATION
- ○ WATCH A MOVIE
- ○ CUDDLE A PET OR HUMAN
- ○ TRY A NEW RESTAURANT
- ○ MAKE TIME TO READ
- ○ TRY A NEW RECIPE
- ○ NO PHONE 30 MINS BEFORE BED

WORKOUT

- ○ CARDIO   ○ WEIGHT   ○ YOGA
- ○ STRETCH ○ REST DAY ○ OTHER

THINGS THAT MAKE ME HAPPY TODAY

HOURS OF SLEEP (Hours)

☾ ☾ ☾ ☾ ☾ ☾ ☾ ☾
1 2 3 4 5 6 7 8

WATER BALANCE (Glass)

▯ ▯ ▯ ▯ ▯ ▯ ▯ ▯
1 2 3 4 5 6 7 8

MOOD

☹ 😕 😐 🙂 😄
ANGRY TIRED SAD GREAT FUN

Day 6:

- Scripture: The mind governed by the flesh is death, but the mind governed by the Spirit is life and peace (Romans 8:6).
- Meditation (Minimum 10 min.)- 1st five minutes (only give thanks); 2nd five minutes (ask Jesus for what you need)
- Self-love Act- Hug yourself real tight. Call your name and tell yourself you love you. (For example, Kasona, I love you; but most of all God loves you).
- Listen to song while dressing: Youtube- I'm Coming Out by Dianna Ross
- Lunch break: Youtube 10 Minute Video- Attitude is Everything| Change Your Attitude| Change Your Life- Inspirational and Motivational Video by Above Inspiration
- Worksheet: Mindful Coloring Mindful Positive Quote I Can Do This
- Bedtime Scripture: Strengthen the feeble hands, steady the knees that give way; say to those with fearful hearts, "Be strong, do not fear; your God will come, he will come with vengeance; with divine retribution, he will come and save you (Isaiah 35: 3-5).
- Positive Quote: Lord, help me to shut out the noise, the distractions in my mind and focus on you. (Bishop Curtis Simmons)

WATERING YOUR GARDEN: 7 DAY ACTIVITY BOOK

Mindful Coloring

Day 7:

- Scripture: But we all, with open face beholding as in a glass the glory of the Lord, are changed into the same image from glory to glory, even as by the Spirit of the Lord (2 Corinthians 3:18).
- Meditation (Minimum 10 min.)- 1st five minutes (only give thanks); 2nd five minutes (ask Jesus for what you need)
- Self-love Act- Hug yourself real tight. Call your name and tell yourself you love you. (For example, Kasona, I love you; but most of all God loves you).
- Listen to Song While Dressing: Youtube- I'm So Glad by Sister Nena Laughton by CalledOut1955
- Lunchbreak: Youtube 10 Minute Motivational Video- Zig Ziglar's Speech Will Leave You Speechless| One of the Most Eye-Opening Speeches Ever by Motivation Hub
- Worksheet: Bingo Self Care Project- Green
- Bedtime Scripture: Peace I leave with you; my peace I give you. I do not give to you as the world gives. Do not let your hearts be troubled and do not be afraid (John 14:27).
- Positive Quote: Where there is a Will, then there is a Way. (Bishop Eugene Rice)

WATERING YOUR GARDEN: 7 DAY ACTIVITY BOOK

Self Care Project Bingo

Put on face mask	Read self-improvement book	Donate unused belongings	Journal routinely for a month	Clean out your room
Making DIY project	Paint	Make a goal list	Eat in fancy resturant	Exercise
Take a nap	Drink more water	Free	Video call your bestfriend	Write 5 things you love about yourself
Spend more time with family	Eat more fruits and vegetables	Go for a walk	Watch a funny movie	Take a selfie
Try out new recipe	Listen to TED talks	Elimininate toxic friends	Go to bed 30 minutes early	Mention 3 things you are grateful for before bed

www.reallygreatsite.com

Congratulations, you finished! In closing, let us continue this journey together. Let us be helpers to one another. We never know what anyone is going through. If we cannot help, let us not tear one another down. One thing that we can all do to help one another is pray for one another. Lord help us to L-O-V-E. That is be longsuffering, be overcomers, be victorious, and be everlasting. Let us remember that God is Love and without His Spirit we cannot truly L-O-V-E because we are all human. Indeed, our MINDS must be transformed for growth to take place whether it be spiritually or naturally. May God continue to bless us and keep us in perfect peace while there is so much turmoil in the world that we live in.

Made in the USA
Columbia, SC
22 December 2023